Legendary Acts

Legendary Acts

JOHN OWER

Athens
The University of Georgia Press

Copyright © 1977 by the University of Georgia Press
Athens, Georgia 30602

Set in 10 on 12 point Monticello type
Printed in the United States of America

Library of Congress Cataloging in Publication Data

Ower, John.
  Legendary acts.
  I. Title.
PS3565.W584L4   811'.5'4   76-49157
ISBN 0-8203-0413-1

Acknowledgments

The author and the publisher gratefully acknowledge permission to reprint these poems which originally appeared in the publications here noted:

"A Bowl of Ripe Fruit" and "Dialogue" were first published in the *Sewanee Review* 83 (fall 1975). Copyright 1975 by the University of the South. Reprinted by permission of the editor.

"New Zealand" and "Night Walk in Winter" were first published in the *Cimarron Review* no. 23 (April 1973) and no. 26 (January 1974). Copyright 1973 and 1974 by the Board of Regents for Oklahoma State University. Reprinted by permission.

"The Example," "Fern Hollow," "The Suicides," and "Two Prayers," *Southern Poetry Review;* "Primeval Story," *Wisconsin Review;* "To His Pregnant Wife," *Southern Humanities Review;* "The Passionate Technician to His Love," and "The Ballad of Jim Randal," *South Carolina Review;* "Alert," *Mississippi Review;* "Hoodoos," *Wind;* "Thunderstorm: Chickamauga Battlefield," and "The Hole in the Road," *University of Windsor Review;* "Sarto's Last Sketch," *Ontario Review;* "Fire-Ant Follies," *Dekalb Literary Arts Journal;* "The Snake-Hunter," *Sandlapper;* "Dowson's Inferno," *Canadian Forum;* "The Sunken Band," "Stripping Small Cicadas," "Landscape for Passion," "A Story for my Daughter," "Paradise," and "After," *Antigonish Review;* "Legendary Act," *Aspen Anthology;* "The Punishment," *Ariel;* "The Legacy," *Epos;* "A Villanelle of the New Minstrels," and "To an Insect in Amber," *Poem;* "Announcement," *Bitterroot;* "The Lice-Pickers," *Sun & Moon;* "Nursery Rhyme," *New Laurel Review;* "Rapunzel's Latest Lover," *Texas Quarterly.*

This book is for Patricia, the household muse,
and for Eli, Vincent and Paul, the poets-in-residence.

Contents

IV: BEAUTY AND THE BEAST

V: TWICE-TOLD TALES

VI: SOME FIRST AND LAST THINGS

VII: MISCELLANIES

I
Eros

Message for Mother's Day

Too curious to know
Exactly what you were,
I didn't use the shield
And you turned my heart to stone.
But that was small loss
Seeing I had faced
The snake in any woman.
Snicker-snack!—
My blade cut off your head,
Its vipers spitting venom,
And I had your witch's power.
Now with winged shoes
And my true self
Invisible as glass
I skim above existence.
The armour-piercing sword
That hangs from my thigh
And that brilliant mirror
Showing every man his image,
Are not better weapons
Than the sordid bag
That, as a party trick,
I open for a girl.

Fern Hollow

The farm, that trough of rustic innocence,
Was where the fairy child would gaze, intense

In meditation on the thing that hung
From stallions, and the effluence of dung,

The heats and bloody afterbirths of cows,
The appetites of litter-eating sows,

And mulled that greater mystery, shut from sight,
The bestial squealing of the springs at night.

Rapunzel's Latest Lover

Love-lorn, and yet aware of some weird power,
He kneels beneath her glinting granite tower.
His heart alight, his bowels a maze of flame,
But with cold feet, he screams her hunnish name.
A muffled thump, and more than half-afraid,
He climbs the twisting snakes of weighty braid.
Of course there follow giggles, groans of pleasure—
The usual witch's stew—then fatal leisure.
As self-contained as an unopened rose,
Rapunzel strikes her favourite Goya pose,
And grins to see her sleeping lover twitch
And grimace, dreaming of a wicked witch.
He starts and sees her moonlit face, age-old
And snow-white in its frame of chilly gold;
The icy blueness of her glacier eyes
Makes every hair upon his body rise.
He waits until she folds in happy sleep,
Then softly to her fatal casement creeps;
He fumbles at his throat a little while,
Then springs into the blackness with a smile.
Rapunzel snaps from dreams of fresh desire,
Her brilliant scalp a sudden mass of fire;
Yanked from her bed, her buxom figure bumps
The bedroom floor, and something distant thumps.
Instantly, she knows the thrilling worst,
Since this has been repeated from the first.
Excited as a child, she runs to see
Crumpled in a ring of thorny trees,
Her leman, with a mask of black despair,
Dead in a hangman's noose of her bright hair.

A Theft of Fire

When man was first made
God omitted wings
For His own good reasons.
So greedy Adam sent his tame dove
To steal fire from heaven.
She lighted at the hearth
Where cherubim were kindled
And gulped a little coal;
Her breast grew iridescent
And her droppings almost whitewash.
She fluttered in excitement back to the earth
And set a huge ruby, glowing purple,
At the tip of Adam's rod.
The man said "Oh!"
In an almost pained surprise,
And quickly tried to quench it in his wife
Who knew nothing yet of nakedness.
As his heat hissed home, a little spark
Lodged in her folds:
Her face lit with a sudden smile of knowledge.
Now when Adam feels
His poker cherry-red,
Or Eve her tiny ember dying down,
They use one another
In the most outrageous fashion.

The Passionate Technician to His Love

Come, be my love, and slip into my cage
And I will keep you watered, warm and fed;
Safe from microbes, being rudely bred;
Quite sanitized from suffering and age.

One evening you will slip into my spell,
Lulled by my anesthetizer's kiss;
Then, in that ether-scented sleep of bliss,
Have probes inserted in your pleasure cells.

My contacts anchored firm in your fair locks,
I'll scan your least desire on my bright screens
And, feeding passion through my pulse-machines,
Rouse you into brainstorms with my shocks.

Landscape for Passion

The weather has a last sultry fling
Before eugenic winter
Can sterilize the land.
The muggy air sweats their starched morals
To a clinging limpness,
While the yellow weeds beckon them to ditches,
To the rank nets where crickets
Fling their last lyrics to the wind.
The bitter apples hang ripe for picking
And the sun winks behind a bank of cloud.
But most of all the maples,
That flare like burning paper, touch their blood
To trigger love in cow-ripened pastures
Or stiff, unchanging pines.

Dialogue

"Love might be like a loaded gun . . ."
      "Or like a bleeding wound . . ."
"Suppose it scalds like summer sun . . ."
      "Or chills like winter ground . . ."

"Love might break me," said the bride;
      "Or drain me," cried the groom;
But soon she compromised with life,
      He parleyed with the tomb.

A Bowl of Ripe Fruit

Not this attack, maybe, but certainly the next:
His ancient face is loose and bluish grey,
With a glint of white whisker in the sun.
After their quick kiss,
As cold and wet as fish,
She sees her father lying in his coffin
A stiff man of wax.

Hypnotized she listens
To the sharp, dry, insistent
Ticking of his clock.
The only sun that shines
In the cold parlour
Is a bowl of ripe fruit.

She imagines Africa
Its sun rising like a ripe orange,
That casts zebra stripes, leopard spots,
On a lion-colored soil.
She imagines men tall as walking trees,
Their thin, angled bodies
Carved from black wood.

She remembers her lover's last kiss,
His face like the sun at the equator;
The push dark and hard as ebony.
Cautiously, like a native dagger,
She unsheathes his last letter.

But a sharp, dry, insistent cough recalls
Her father's kiss, cold as a snow-man's:
She spreads a white cloth across the ripe fruit;
And consigns her dark god
To his flat rag coffin.

The Ballad of Jim Randal

"O where have ya bin, Jim Randal, my hun?
O where have ya bin, my handsum young man?"
"Mind yer own business, an' mak my bed soon,
Fer I'm hungry fer luvin' an' fain wad lie doon."

"But the kettle is boilin', Jim Randal, my hun!
An' yer supper is spoilin', my handsum young man!"
"Toss the lot to the dog, luver, mak my bed soon,
Fer I'm hungry fer luvin' an' fain wad lie doon."

"But there's grease on yer shirt, Jim Randal, my hun!
Yer unseamin' my skirt, my handsum young man!"
"Stitch it up with yer tongue, luver, mak my bed soon,
Fer I'm hungry fer luvin' an' fain wad lie doon."

"Yer bitin' like sin, Jim Randal, my hun!
Yer breakin' the skin, my handsum young man!"
"Blood's thicker than tea, luver, mak my bed soon,
Fer I'm hungry fer luvin' an' fain wad lie doon."

"Don't tell me yer done, Jim Randal, my hun!
I've hardly begun, my handsum young man."
"I'm starvin' fer steak, luver, fetch me some soon,
Fer I only had stout an' a sandwich at noon."

Geography of Love

I once loved a blonde:
By night she seemed the sun that never sets
In a polar June,
By day she was the moon that mocks its winter.
Her flesh was now ice, now fire
To my abstracted lust.
Then I loved a black
For what seemed the tropic of her loins;
First, a flood of butterflies and fruit,
Then crocodiles.
Now wiser, I would love
In a temperate zone of fact,
Where contraries kiss
In the spring and autumn;
Where the white of apple-blossom
Is qualified by scarlet,
And its fruit is matured
To a blood-red ripeness
By a touch of frost.

To His Pregnant Wife

All the little Eves
(So that eternal optimist
My male ego hopes)
Proffer their ripe apples.
And you, my wife, are swelling
Like a pomegranate,
Or that Pandora's box
A wasp's nest in summer.
Alas, the little man
That sums up the hungers of the flesh
Is lively as the child
That kicks in your belly;
Conceived in Adam's sin,
Even he is fed
By a snake that winds inside.
But set your heart at rest:
That primeval upstart, the serpent,
Bears around his crown
The wound of the little crucifixion.
Now, sanctified, my Old Adam sleeps
As peacefully as Jesus with the beasts.

II
A small and secular confessional

The Hole in the Road
(Auckland, New Zealand)

When I was a child,
There was a hole in the road
That kept reappearing;
A collapse in our carefully levelled way
With edges jagged as a shark's jaw.
It dated, so my grandfather said,
(An ancient joker wise in all lore)
From the time when the city was volcanoes,
When lava had erupted
From the bottom of the sea.

Crews of dark men
With a roaring pitch machine,
An iron bull with fire in its belly,
Cursed, and fed it gravel by the ton,
But nothing kept its grinning
Gape closed for long.
I used to stand and stare,
Fascinated by its black recess,
And by the Styx that tinkled
Just out of sight:
It was like the evening sea
That swallowed up the sun.

Once it was big enough
For me to walk inside—
My grandmother screamed,
And ran to pull me back
To my fury and relief.

Once, although safely tucked in bed,
I dreamed it came and swallowed up our house:
Soon enough my grandparents died.

A Story for my Daughter

When I was only five
My granddaddy led me
To the family closet,
Where the skeletons of namesakes for nine generations
Clattered on their hangers, and the ghosts of their women
Squeaked like vermin
At the edge of the light.
My grandfather's hold was like the clamp of a trap;
"Stand put," he said, with the smile of the sun
That hung ice in bright fangs and daggers
From his frozen eaves.
He fumbled in the black for a second,
And then began to haul out an endless iron chain.
It looped like a snake
But with an iron clank
Of its links like a machine.
At last it went taut from its hidden end,
And grandfather pulled until his face went purple;
I was scared that he would drop
Of a stroke upon the spot.
Then, out rumbled like an earthquake from the dark
An iron ball as heavy
As the heart of the world.
It squatted as definitive as two coming suicides
And sundry other deaths.
"Hold still," he hissed, in a tone that froze my muscles
While he locked the manacle
Around my thin leg.
"This is your inheritance," he said with an eye
Like the North Star on a sub-zero night.

Then he dropped the key
In his breast pocket
To be warmed by his heart that creaked with a vengeance
To bear its heavy load.

The Suicides

In the cold Humboldt current of my dreams,
Night after night, I fish for three suicides
That angle for me also.
Beneath a sky with the icy polish
Of volcanic glass,
In which uncharted constellations glitter
Like the Argus eyes of God,
They rise, one by one, through black water.
Each has ten
Gigantic white arms
That insinuate and stretch
In their anguish to ensnare me.
Half as a sop, and half in cunning,
I bait my triple-pointed hooks of steel
With my own guts as an enticement.
The beaks clash like enormous scissors
With hunger for my vitals.
Glittering with sweat from head to toe,
One by one, I haul my horrors home.
Then, with the break of day flashing
Like blood or fire from my brilliant axe,
I section the cadavers
As dead as white rubber.
I chop each corpse into a hundred neat pieces,
Which I fling one by one into the waves,
As my peace-offering
To sleek, primeval sharks.

The Legacy

My grandfather willed me
An ancient railway watch;
Primeval and heavy, a fossil from the days
When locomotives guzzled tons of water,
And digested hard coal by the car.
They huffed and they rumbled
Like brontosauruses,
As they pushed history
Across a continent.
The watch, with its case of burnished steel,
Seemed built to last forever.
Its guts, relentless as the breed of men
That swallowed up the West,
Still kept perfect time.
After I had listened to it tick like a bomb
Through a night of dinosaurs, I thought of pawning it
To buy a steak dinner, but some dark respects
Kept me from catering
To petty appetites.
Then, at a display
Of treasures rifled from the earth
I saw the shark's tooth.
It was six inches long,
A brilliant jet, like anthracite,
And flawless as the day that it fell, disregarded,
From the monster's mouth into the blackness
That swallows history.
Nearby lay the wicked spearpoints
That polished off mammoth
From the continent.

The tooth had greater length,
Nor was it shaped, chip by petty chip,
Through organic curves;
Its saw edges angled
Straight to the point.
Its perfect surface, smooth as rouged steel,
Played with my image.
Well, the price we pay for revelations
Is sometimes proportional
To their true extent.
Now grandfather's watch
Captures the sun in a hockshop window
With the silly switchblades and crude .38s.
The usurping tooth hangs
From its steel chain,
A dark momento of the size of time,
And primal generations.

Desert Nightmare

Down the desert track
Was a train of dead creatures,
Beheaded in strict order of their size,
Then dropped in white sand.
My eye, unattuned
To creation's finer details,
Picked up the path
With a fat black scarab;
But it took a quick succession
Of a streamlined lizard,
A racer and a rabbit,
Their swiftness spilt like water,
To impel the message home.
Next was a coyote, with his coward tail
Tucked between his legs.
Floating in the cool
Lucidity of dreams,
I traced the chain of lifeless beings back
To a fruit-fly torso
At the edge of nothing.
Then, turning in my tracks,
I pursued the littered trail,
Past the limp coyote,
Strangely free of flies.
At last, crucified upon a cactus tree,
Was a decapitated god.
His toppled head, the first one I saw,
Bore my own image.

III

Up above, in between, and downunder

Alert*

Here our longitudes converge
And lines of latitude emerge.

The Eskimo, whose common sense
Was his first line of self-defense,

Found it blizzard-swept and bare
And left it to the wolf and hare.

We, more resourceful and more bold,
Send surrogates to battle cold;

To wage a long and losing fight
Of sanity with frozen night.

We, by default left malcontent
With the wrong half-continent,

Locked in snug suburban tombs
Where only bourgeois blessings bloom,

Are irresistibly inclined
Towards our North to be defined,

In darkness, cold and ice to see
Shadows of our nullity,

*Canadian Forces Base: the most northerly inhabited point on the globe

In lives hermetically enclosed
Our mortal fear: to be exposed;

And, like half-buried mammoth bones,
Our scattered myths, chilled hard as stones.

Night Walk in Winter

Beyond the parked couples
Trees close around:
One must always look behind.

Perhaps an owl will strike with icy claws,
There are feathers here to prove him.

Perhaps a big dog
Will recall his wild blood.

But always only silence and the cold,
Moonlight and loneliness.

Then at turning point a fallen tree
Stripped by starving hares.

From Canada to New Zealand

Twenty years after my fall, I sometimes remember the garden,
Though an angel once tilted my world, and now I live in winter:
Frost on the window-pane for ferns,
And waist-deep snow for pasture.
Yet sometimes I recall November lilies,
Whiter than drifts in the ditches, or a hillside of nasturtiums,
Whose growth ran riot like fire before the wind.

There is no cherub banning my return
With a burning sword; only a sad, wise serpent
Who whispers in my ear how everything would be different,
How I could no longer look through ingenuous eyes.

Thunderstorm: Chickamauga Battlefield

The sun in September
Is pitiless as summer,
The thunderstorms still hidden
In a mask of haze.
A buzzard soars and soars
In the teeth of the weather
Till death is just a speck
In the nondescript grey.

The visitor will not discover corpses
Depending from the pines like Christmas baubles,
The skeletons and snakes
Lie dozing in the grass.

Without a moment's warning
Sounds a cannonade
And the landscape is shattered
By the grapeshot of hail.

Mighty Oaks . . .

In Chattanooga everybody
Kept a vicious dog;
The only place for lovers
Was a battlefield
Where more than twenty thousand died
In the Civil War.
Just before we flew
To a cleaner hemisphere
We used to wander sadly through the woods
And note by the markers
How many perished
On each spot of ground.
One day we came across an oak
That was ancient when the grapeshot hissed:
It was as old as the Fall.
Its branches were festooned with mistletoe
Like a Druid tree.
We picked up an acorn to plant downunder,
But then I was afraid that it might carry some disease
And so I tossed it in a muddy stream.
In a new hemisphere, nothing happens
Except the traffic's wild
And the girls wear next to nothing;
But in the smoky bars, on Friday nights,
Pakehas and Maoris
Sing very different songs.
By the dark Waikato, in a park,
A rusty gunboat, brim-full of silt,
Commemorates the founding of the town.
Right now, it beds inconsequential flowers,
But river-silt is rich, and I am sorry
That we did not smuggle in our little seed.

New Zealand

This paradise that never was—
It takes forever getting here
Anyhow from anywhere.
Arrived, one finds a little bit of England
From the Eisenhower age,

Yet it is very much its own place;
Like Lilliput, perhaps, with some reforms
And no standing war.

Even the big brother who made good
Is standoffish. See

The northern island lunging like a shark
That would eat its southern fellow whole.
Below, the roaring forties, and the pole.

A Natural History of Kiwi Academe

Downunder academics meet
In solemn luncheon sausage round;
The talk is dry, the sherry sweet,
The headaches are, at least, profound.

Like Ruapehu, elders humble
Mortals with expansive mass,
Though near extinction, still they rumble
Little puffs of ash and gas.

Straw Yankee scholars are reproved,
Sound British judgements ballast lunch,
In emerald fields, not far removed,
Self-satisfied, the milk-cows munch.

They know their pedigree is pure
As B.A., Auckland; Ox. B.Litt.,
And as they amble, graze the ground
With weighty butter-fatted tit.

The moa was a mighty bird
Of mythy days when monsters walked,
It earthquaked when he dropped a turd
And hurricaned each time he squawked—

And so we pass to the deceased—
From bits of bone dredged out of bogs
Primeval skeletons are pieced
With pedant care. Like kauri logs

Whose girth encircles centuries,
Whose grain stays sound in sodden mud
Bulk these immortal memories
Embalmed alive by gummy blood.

Visit to Pirongia

Puffily we climb
Up the dead volcano,
Past happy cows.
A new runt calf
Crouches by a hedge;
Then the sudden bush.
Huge pigeons whizz like apparitions
In the first and last clearing;
Just a hundred yards from lambs
All direction dies.
We stumble over logs, peer through thickets
Towards running water
That we cannot see.
A tui's purity
Mocks all we are—
O sweet singer, native happy here,
You lure us to loss in a jungle
As tangled as our minds.
But when in dreams did jew's-ears crinkle
In this sodden brown translucent
Caricature of flesh?
What psychosis made these epiphytes
Drop as strong as hanging ropes or burst
In sprays of leaves like cruel erotic daggers?
The sun begins to set,
Past time to strike the trail,
And break out at last where a pre-romantic haze
Softens down the valley.
Back home you glower in the dusk,
Sombre-crowned mountain

With your cloud-catching jags;
Twenty miles away you rise as a reminder
That to keep death at distance
It must stay in one eye,
Above a near horizon.

IV
Beauty and
the beast

Sarto's Last Sketch

All day I have prickled
With my jealousy.
Should I make you faithful
With this stiletto,
Honed to a tip
That would slit your white throat
Without a trace of feeling?
Sit, my exquisite pencil point
In a thousand sharp strokes upon the paper
Will capture you as no lover can.

The Snake-Hunter

In seeking snakes, I strip bark from pines,
Roll logs, watch startled life scuttle;
But prying in the dark cracks of nature
Yields lower life only.
Snakes always slip
Into the corner of the eye
An adventitious loveliness.

Dowson's Inferno

I'd rather be reborn a swine or frog
Than live like this: a prostitute's small dog.

To feel her fingers snake along my spine,
And hear her vicious tongue hiss she is mine,

To press my puny member at her bust
And lick her neck to titillate her lust,

Then, just before the blossom of our sin,
Swept under her sway bed, when customers slink in.

The Sunken Band

Some place where the cold gulls cry,
Miller and his band lie drowned;
And yet I sometimes wonder, when the sun returns
To light the northern sky with long pale day,
Whether the sunbeams might not filter down,
And strike the bones, so they begin to play
With that old ebullient sound
To make the fishes and the seaweed sway.
And if we heard, could we not lose our sense
With longing to be clean again, and free
And drive like lemmings to that freezing sea
To drown with our dead innocence.

A Villanelle of the New Minstrels

We eaglets found the nest of peace a bore;
Security was clotted with our dung,
We screeched to try our little wings at war.

Born ravenous, our only call was "More!"
Though innocence like bits of eggshell clung,
We eaglets found the nest of peace a bore.

And soon we saw sweet wounds our mother tore
In snow-white rabbits as they brightly sprung,
We screeched to try our little wings at war.

At dusk, we screamed to see the crimson pour
From a sun that heaven's talons hung;
We eaglets found the nest of peace a bore.

And with such knowledge, nothing could restore
The whistle at the tip of callow tongue,
We screeched to try our little wings at war.

Now at our death, exalted by our gore,
We pass without a silly swansong sung;
We eaglets found the nest of peace a bore,
We screeched to try our little wings at war.

Stripping Small Cicadas

Stripping small cicadas is a game
For innocents, below remorse or shame.
The quarry is instinctual, stingless, weak;
One only needs the strategy to sneak
To striking distance, patience to outwait
The small defense of silence, then the fate
Is sealed with one quick snatch. Now rip the wings
And cripple one more idiot that sings.

Fire-Ant Follies

A fire-ants' nest
Is one of those realities
Into which a poem sinks
Like water into sand.
Never mind, insecticide
Can still contain disorder.
The poison burbles like a line of verse
In the Shangrila tongue
As, in pure potency,
It leaves the flashing can.
This time, not a drop defiles
The still pond where the caddis worms
Weave their works of art from nature's trash
And then are metamorphosed
To fly fine as spirits.
Overnight the ants
Tunnel with a secret
Guerilla discipline.
Their nursery offends,
A little breast of Babel.
With an angry kick
I activate their chaos,
Jumbling the hopes
Of coming generations:
The pale amorphous grubs, new kings and queens gifted
With luminescent wings.
As I administer
A dose of discipline,
Stings open like a lotus bud
In instant Buddhist vision.

The dropped can takes a bright tumble
And spills its mortal magic on the water.
Soon little fishes jump
In fuddled ecstacy,
Creating perfect rings.
Thus am I defeated;
Too soon the royal pairs
Will exercise their heritage of flight.
They will flicker in the clear September sun,
Sparks from an unextinguished hearth.

Legendary Act

The ghost of Sophie Tucker entertains
In the nightclub of the shades.
Alone among the dead
It is she who keeps her voice;
It permeates Hades
With its raw perfume.
Persephone titters, and her groin of ivory
Moistens with the scented
Ichor of the gods.
Her lord's frown relents
As she strokes his grim sickle;
His marble haunches shift with pleasure to the lay
And rock his iron throne.
Even the shadows
Are fluttering and twittering
Like bats in sudden light.
Alas, despite their cocktails
Of sacrificial blood,
They have less body
Than the voice that dies exhausted
Into primal night.

A Poem for Owen Warland

Nothing but a dust-mote
To the crass eye,
And yet through the loupe
The perfect piece of art.
With antennae finer
Than thinnest gold wire
She tickles out her way.
Her miniscule eyes
Flame from a myriad
Of prismatic facets:
It is as though Spinoza
Had learned to work diamond.
No stretching of the glassblower's craft
Could vein her crystal wings.
She delicately preens
The streamlined abdomen
That tapers to a needle
Ten times more tenuous
Than a hair spring.
With the assurance
Of the miniaturist tracing
Brows with a brush
Of one camel hair,
She stabs her own egg into the egg
Of a grosser parasite
And saves a butterfly.

Rimbaud's Last Poem

All my adolescent
Pustules are now dry.
Yet once I had such painful joy
To squirt their mortal seed
Upon my own dark image
In my mother's bedroom mirror.
No more small volcanoes
Of impassioned manifesto
Boil up from the Phlegethon
Of my corrupted blood.
Now, at best, a petty zit
Yields a fine white worm of death,
Or a thwarted hair
Beneath my bourgeois collar
Festers like the poison snake
Of poetry betrayed.
Shall I recall my Muses
By kicking off my shoes,
And walking, naked-toed as Adam,
In this crimson mud?
Then I should have that pleasure,
More filthy than my lice,
Of having some black urchin pick
With his exquisite thorn
To stir the chigger-eggs that brood
Beneath my horny nails.

Foresight

Goya chafes at the door
Like a black bull ready for the ring.
He sees red with jealousy, an unmarried man
With a sprouting forehead, but far worse than that
He is horny and impatient.
He waits for a snorting matador
To sink his weapon home to the heart
Of the celebrated nude.
Her lust, over-ripe as Pasiphaë's desire,
Drives her down to snuffle on all fours:
The breasts droop like udders as her bull-man bores.
Her breath becomes asthmatic, and Goya thinks of blood
Exploding from the holes that cruel horns gore.
Then, in a flash, he fantasizes
Beyond the impalements and dismemberments of war:
There, at the centre of his crimson vision,
Floats Picasso's Minotaur.

On a Photograph of Bix Beiderbecke

A Freudian would say
That the penetrating stare
Is really meant for mama,
That the manhood that he clutches
In his right hand
Ends in a nipple and a womb.
Thus, the sound that came
"Like a girl saying yes"
Was merely involution of frustration.
Obviously, liquor bottles gave
His lips their highest pleasure:
Hence, the male lover.

But perhaps the age that made
Lionel a legend
Could speak better to this haunted picture:

"With wings concealed and pinned
By his ridiculous tuxedo,
He clasps his silver trumpet as he stares
Through the speakeasy's haze
And the casual flappers
With a seraph's sharp vision.
Although trapped and tortured
In a brazen labyrinth,
His soul made music,
Played upon by some sublime fingers,
As it wormed its way to Heaven."

In this interpretation, bath-tub gin
Was the only fellow-spirit
That his crass time provided.

Performance

We take a butterfly
And tear off its right front wing;
We take a ballerina
And nail her left foot to the floor.
We say to the insect,
"Silly cripple, fly."
We tell the ballerina
To dance despite the nail:
See, see,
They do it brilliantly.

V
Twice-told tales

The Punishment

The fate of the suitors
Was not as Homer told.
After having strangled
The smart-ass son,
They gang-banged Penelope,
And then for variety
Raped Eurycleia.
They hunted down Eumaeus
With his own hounds,
Cut off his balls
And tossed them to the pigs.
Next, for a kick,
At a drunken feast
They pulped an old beggar
And found it was Odysseus
By his scarred thigh.
To round off the job
They soaked his old dog
In olive oil, and put a torch to him.
By this time the pickings
Were getting pretty slim,
So they burnt down the house
With the servants in it,
And headed for their homes.
Zeus, the all-seeing,
With a grim smile,
Unleashed the subtle Erinye of boredom.

The Real Johnny Appleseed

Oh don't be so romantic—
I kept a proper schedule,
Arriving on cue
At each new settlement
As sure as death and taxes.
The farmer whose soil
I selected for my seed
Was seen as one accurst,
For from a second bag
At my hand sinister
With special care I culled
Burdocks, thistles,
And a pair of rattlesnakes.

The Tortoise and the Hare

Like the fabled hare
I shivered at the starting line,
Running muscles toned
As the finest steel spring.
Then, in my innocence,
Thinking time a greyhound,
I jumped at the word
In fear and exaltation.
Soon, I stole a glance,
Saw nothing but my dust
Behind me like a ghost.
And so I left the road
To nibble at sweet shoots
And sniff the mazy ways
Of the rabbits in the meadow.
Meanwhile time,
That stolid old tortoise
With a cold purpose
In his primeval eye,
Was plodding foot by foot
Towards my finish line.

The Last Circle

Judas always was
A level-headed sort:
He thought Jesus was a great talker,
But a little bit off
With that stuff about love.
Still, there's always money in religion
As his best deal proved.
He invested the payoff
In a small corner bar,
And pimped two Magdalenes
From an upper room;
He was soon an arch-respectable
Publican and sinner.
He died as he had lived, without regrets,
At a ripe old age,
For unlike crazy Peter,
He never was the type to have hangups.

VI
Some first and last things

Primeval Story

A butterfly blasphemed,
And was degraded to a stone;
The rock implored God
To restore its hue and motion.
The Creator's magic touch
Stretched it to a supple S;
His finger-tips lit
Brilliant bands along its length.
As a little extra touch of love,
God endowed his new creature
With a soft voice.
There lay, hissing out its thanks,
The first coral snake.

Paradise

In the latest Eden,
There are no Jewish jokes;
No one's even heard
Of Abraham or Moses.
There are no more vulgar pokes at sex;
Liberated Eve
Aborted Cain and Abel.
There aren't any wisecracks
Arising from the grave,
And no hands are dirty
With the red clay.
There are certainly no naughty gestures
Behind Jehovah's back;
Everybody thinks
He's a sweet old soul.
The serpent is coiled
As stiff as stone with boredom;
The apple falls rotten from the tree,
But for some reason God
No longer walks in His garden.

Orange Tree

I raise golden suns
From the cold earth
At the dark of the year
When death touches birth.
As bitter as myrrh
Are my sun's skin and seeds,
But sweet as frankincense
The cup its flesh bleeds.
In Holy Land I lift
Suns so man may see
Both Cross and Resurrection
At God's Nativity.

Two Prayers

I

Lord, that my soul
Were like the coconut
With a husk of fibres
Tough enough to bear
The fall from that green nest
That was half-way to heaven.
Lord, that the shell of my spirit
Were impervious to seal
The milk of innocence
At its rich heart.
Then even my blind eyes
Would find the good soil
Like the seed of wheat.
My trunk would soon soar
In hosannas to the sun.

II

Lord, allow my soul, like the cicada
To rise from the tree-roots
That snake into the soil.
Lord, let my flight
Be straight into your light,
And even the split shell
That, winged, I leave hanging
Upon a rough trunk
Be a little work of wonder.

To an Executive with Ulcer

For the selling of your soul
You bear the Beast's mark, Cain's brand,
In your poor tummy-tum.
When God plays wit
He's always metaphysical;
His justice is poetic.
To begin with, your wound lies closer
To your balls than your brains,
Still closer to the scissors
That cut you off from mummy.
Perhaps, like the pelican,
You feed the foul squawking
Nest of your compulsions
With your own blood,
Or perhaps your heart has dropped
From fear into your stomach.
Maybe God has armed
The head of the serpent
That coils in your bowels
With a stinger to destroy you;
Perhaps He just sent a coal from Hell.
At any rate, you got
No proud red forehead,
In taking such pains for your pains—
Why, even the blushes
Are hidden in your stomach—
(Don't bite your nails,
It's hard on the ulcer.)

Progress

Of all of the tunnels
That twist through the night
The only one that rises
To the surface is triangular
And just three feet
From its base to disappearance.
To advance, one must at least
Drop upon his knees,
But even then the head,
Puffed up with knowledge,
Still catches at the point.
Needless to say
We have become troglodytes,
Our eyes having atrophied
To two pink spots
That warn against the light.
What ultimate realities
We shall at last discover
As we burrow down and down
Have yet to be revealed.

Hoodoos

Those odd rock goblins in the desert
Are not the last remains
Of stylite saints transmuted into monuments.
Nor are they memorials to some silly gossips
Who couldn't quite resist
Seeing God obliterate neighbors in a Sodom
Long since ashes under sand.
What you see eroded into such grotesques
As never graced cathedral,
Are doubters astonished
By what blossomed after rain.

Announcement

Ladies and gentlemen, your flight
Is just about to crash.
This is a good news/
Bad news joke.
The bad news is the helpless terror
That becomes the daily bread of modern man.
For good news, even death by burning
Is a great deal quicker
Than the creeping flame of cancer.
Seen from this perspective
Even the bomb
Is not, perhaps, unmixed with blessing.
The temperature for those
Who are about to land in Hell
Is as sharp as ever.
In Heaven, where the fire is pure light,
There is neither heat nor cold:
Have a happy death.

The Desert

Here Paradise is nothing
But the mad fantasy
Of men who die for water;
Here everything is thorns.
Here the sun rises
To a burning zenith
From the blood red rock.
Here every valley
Deprived of even shadow
Is the pit at noon.
Here God will quarry
The semi-precious stones
Of the last city.

VII
Miscellanies

Phoenix in July

People grill their toast
In the morning sun.
At noon mad dogs
Forget their hydrophobia
While the poor Englishmen,
Their cool boiled to steam,
Savage passers-by.
By six the saguaro
Abandon prickled dignity
And bow down for mercy.
Meanwhile Apache,
Done with reservations,
Are buried like snakes
Beneath the desert sand.
More patient than the Camelback
They wait for the moon.

Faculty Senate

The conclave of maggots
Converges at the juicy
Centre of the flap.
Though its edges are becoming
Perhaps a little dry,
Still there is hope
That some brighter spirits
May graduate as flies.
O winged administrators
Of viruses and eggs,
To you we burn sacrifice
In your approved fashion.
Forgive us if the smoke
Is perhaps a little rancid
And savours of revolt.
Your all-seeing eyes
With their thousand facets
Will penetrate the smother
To see our true subservience.

After

When serpents can reduplicate
All their most subtle twists,
How odd that the tangled knots of time
Can never be redeemed.

The Juggernaut

Brown, skinny arms and legs shake with the strain;
Feet slither in the treacherous red mud;
Rope-bitten shoulders run with sweat and blood,
Men drag their death with patient, loving pain.

Some fall, yet still the crowd pulls ceaselessly.
At last the brutal cart is at the crest;
Dark eyes are flaming for a moment's rest,
What avatars do such black gemstones see?

With their last breath, they scamper down the hill;
Prostrate themselves across the ruts to give
Breast or head, so that strict god that lives
In the dry wood wheels can drink his fill.

The Example
(after the Mexican poet Miron)

Like a horrid fruit, on view he hung
Rotting near the trunk upon a limb.
Witnessing a law's unlikely whim,
Slowly, like a pendulum, he swung.

The coxcomb tuft of hair, the tongue that poked
Between the lips, the body hanging bare
Of decency, gave him a clownish air.
Beside my horse some urchins laughed and joked.

From the mournful corpse, with its bowed head,
Outrageous on its gibbet, yet still shy,
A stench upon the gusty wind was spread.

With a censer's solemn pace he swung;
The sun was rising in a clear blue sky,
The landscape like the one Tibullus sung.

The Lice-Pickers
(after Rimbaud)

When the child's forehead, full of pins of red,
Implores a swarm of daydreams, vague and pale,
Two tall and charming sisters come beside his bed
Their fragile fingers tipped with silver nails.

Before an open window, where blue air
Bathes a mass of flowers, they seat the child.
As dew is falling in his heavy hair
They move frail fingers, terrified and wild.

He hears the singing of their breath in fright
That smells of long rose honey, hears the hiss
Which interrupts from time to time—their tight
Lips catching spittle, or the urge to kiss.

In scented silence he can hear their black
Eyelashes beat; in tipsy sloth their nice
Electric fingers making little cracks,
As royal nails dispatch the tiny lice.

There rise in him the wine of laziness
And a harmonica's delirious sigh;
The child feels according to how slowly they caress
The ceaseless rise and fall of his desire to cry.

The Smell

The bouquet of success
Was not the faint fragrance
Of his lost mother's skin,
Nor yet the rich scent
Of the spring roses
That he pricked his finger cutting
For a dead love.
Still, it had that special acrid savour
That can tickle even
The chryselephantine
Nostrils of the gods.

To an Insect in Amber

Floating dead still
In a frozen gold sea,
Your frail appendages intact
After centuries,
Do you exhibit
How rigor mortis
Touches immortality?

Or is that elegant
Abandon, as in air,
Nothing but the grimace
Of your stuck despair?

Ant in September

Some of us aspire too high
On silver wings, and doubtless die;

Whereas the sensible and sound
Work, pleasureless, on solid ground.

It's true that our beloved queen
Will positively wax obscene,

Mooning on the lost delight
Of some silly "nuptial flight";

O, she will prattle endlessly
Of fresh horizons she could see,
And penetrating ecstasy;

And then relive the sick despair
As she fluttered from the air,

To shrug away her youth and beauty
And assume the weight of duty.

Personally, if you ask me,
I think it's all just fantasy

That she spins to while away
The intervals from lay to lay,

And, though I mean no disrespect,
Candidly, I do suspect
A slipping of her intellect—

I mean, how could that bloated thing
Have ever risen on the wing?—

For all her fancy talk of flight
She never even sees the light!

But, granted that her tale is true,
What on earth has that to do
With busy bees like me and you?—

See what she finally found was best:
To stay secure inside the nest,
Outproducing all the rest—

It's sad the way she's growing old—
My! Aren't these mornings getting cold?

Nursery Rhyme

The bridge will burn,
The worm will turn,
The dog will have his day:
The best laid plans of mice and men
Rightly go astray.